Published by Lethe Press | lethepressbooks.com

ISBN: 978-1-59021-635-4

This work is fiction, and any resemblance to any real person, dead or otherwise, is incidental.

Typesetting: Ryan Vance
Cover Artist: Piper Day

his salt & her flower

contrite euphoria:
falling deeply, madly, helplessly

Finn Mott

LETHE PRESS

dedicated to

the disenfranchised
the ostracized
the unforgettable
...
those who knownthose who desire more
than the world will give the vulnerable
those who drink the same old coffee
in hopes for a different view
the misunderstood raindrops on a sunny day

prologue

political protrusions / blood transfusions / singular confusions

blue bow ties / *the following is a retry* / at the beloved befriended / belittle belonging

disturbed...

Let ME Be CLEAR: forcing euphoric contrition is the definition of societal insanity, loveless meanders marries immorality, displaced fear is no excuse to abuse

The following was written on a used tissue

fandom

i do not recognize my eyes when i look in the mirror

crying midnights - tossing stones
at melting glaciers
a fragrant of tragedy - scrubbed clean with forgotten
safety regulations
lemon cake

may i have this dance with "alternity"
a salted flower in your ear

into. a. tearful. night.
turning back time - an invisible hand
madly / helplessly (in love) with the malicious /
midnight /
magnificent midnight (fall with me)

-writing in the dark, i have run out of words

two hour parking / too many empty gestures / i miss you, i love you, i am here for you during JUNE! I WILL DO YOU A FAVOR, by pretending to care for 30 days, but as soon at it hits 31 i will go back to the decadent / delicate hatreds that destroy / damage / self destruct these countries' libraries

BANNED. you have been blocked, banned, abandoned, stoned for too long, actually i don't do plant, unless you count the planted systems designed for regression

I don't want to scare you too soon, but i guess i have been scared of myself my whole life because that was what i was TAUGHT. to not understand what is misunderstood and mutated by nature; rather the human is the OPPRESSOR not nature. cause it would be nice if we had a choice to be born BANNED, so i am sorry that i can't be sorry that i am who i am, but i can't just write something that is beautiful. AFTERALL i am not not beautiful, and neither are you. for only in abolition can we see rainbows through thunderstorms, but remember only in JUNE.

i love all my friends but i still don't even like myself.
the six pack did not do what it was supposed to do.
it turns out that you need to love yourself for other
things that are not aesthetically pleasing to the eye
that are still BLINDED by the 7th grade GIFTED and
TALENTED that gave me this PERFECTIONISM
which attaches self worth to tangible comparisons

so i return
to the resume
which can never be comparable to this
shall we resume:
rejection is thy branch of breath on a foggy fall
window
indoors. watching from across the street of an
amusement park

i am not a model, i am a 7 year old chain smoker, but
my lungs are full of the smoke you traded for air
i do not have a perfectly chiseled body
i do not fit the picture

i am here
and for the first time I don't care what you think of me
because
i am me
I AM SENSITIVE/ if you do not like it yo
u can leave/ being broken is a blessing of heatstrokes/
beauty is a   bottomless mug

with no handle/ if you look through
the murky coffee there are visions of the
wandering. wondering. boyhood
delusions/ charred masculine self hatreds/
decadent weeds growing in thrown out plastic in the
deepest. most undiscovered part of the oceans. among
your eyes. grimacing at
the blood droplets frozen in time/
manipulated desires and retired
dreamhoods leaking into the sewer at the bottom of
the Prarie Wood Street. where the divorce started and
never ended . then we all
continue on and pretended that the
dented was brand new. with that
new car smell and 7th grade gifted and

talented.

i may be paranoid but at least i am not forgotten

-Helsinki, Finland -10/07/2022

- foreign nations- same love - tumultuous
thoughts - breathing noises - i have not showered in 5
days - romantic rhythms - i miss the
cold where nothing grows-
-On moonless nights i can't help but
feel alone without my cratered
companion.
when mornings come my way
sugary skin
becomes lost in lost euphoria.
i am lost out here in the start of it all.
i am lost without the moonlight to guide my eyes
through political bargains, personless
pressures, godless love letters.

sundara:

-to be beautiful or handsome

cowboy boots clicking clacking
i deleted all
social media because i am worried about the people
i don't know pretending to know me in the way i am
most deeply afraid of
not here not now
you can't live like this
OBSESSED with oneself

pretending i am confident

so please follow me on tik tok @finn_the_poet

as success dwindles so does
the absentia of humanity
BIG BOY words are for BIG BOYS
stomping my feet

Stavanger, Norway - 10/02/2022

the shocks are all gone in my car, sometimes we take
so many beatings that we just go limp, now every time
i drive my body shakes and my heart aches for the
trauma i put my car through, delicate destructions
intertwined with blood, sweat, and history,
we are just so fantastically fucked.
shucking the corn every day

3:00 AM dew, point me in the correct direction would
you, leave the sensitivity to the men.

wallop - skip - lukewarm rain drips down my
eyebrows, stinging - ringing - you are here not back
there - goosebumps never listen to dry skin - call them
- **euphoric dandelions.**

plaster your face with stickers - stick to everything -
hold on for fleeting fleas buzz - inside my ears a jungle
is infested by humanized deforestation - emotionless
restoration to steel - cement - hard things that boys
are constructed to consume

a little boy told me i talk weird - i told him he talks
weird too

clouds whisper in hushed frequencies,
that one over there across the valley is crying, leaking
from underneath its underbelly, sun dried and diced.

toasting stale cinnamon raisin bagels for dinner,
dipping into rotten blueberry cream cheese, i
consumed the color blue from the minute of birth to
the death of common sense.

slipping sideways - external beauty may be born - inner must be earned - churned upon uneven ground - dripping daylight - generations genetics - THIS IS MY BODY:

there is no such thing as *a way out* - only deeper, under the goosebumps - borders define material persistence - confluence of influence - scroll, swipe, cry, hold hands with granite countertops that my mother never made me sandwiches on to take to elementary school lunch in a brown paper bag that wrinkled by my tiny hands shoving it to the bottom of my backpack that the dog always got into because i never took the leftovers out which hung to the right of the front door of the red house on Capital street after the divorce.

straight lines are a figment of imagination - circle a, b, c or d, or none of the above, or all of the above, or a and b, or a and c, or a and d, or fuck i do not remember.

I CAN'T FEEL MY FACE because i got seasonal
allergies that listen to no constitution
like 'merica'
cause this is America
actually the United States of America
and godless the American Dream with the white
picket fence, and white voice, and capitalism, and
sexism, and racism, and ableism, and homophobia,
and all the other isms and spasms of humanity we
have come to love

but the word love is funny isn't it
for every single time i put my pen to to paper i write
a god damn fucking love poem and i wish that i could
just not be here, so centered on the thing i cannot
control, and what may never belong to me and my
cold blooded hands, those conversion camps that i
drove by on my way back from California where for
the first time in 19 years i saw that maybe there is
more to me than money, a wife, a house, and money,
did i mention money and a wife, and yes a house with
a fence please, preferably white so that i can have some
privacy from all the things that are uncomfortable and
not normal, who made the normal by which we abide,
the one in which i do not and will not fit inside

strangers trying to tell me how to live my life

sometimes i get migraines when i get stressed and
the way i remember how to spell desserts is stressed
backwards; the truth is this is all
sdrawkcab

did you know that our universe is expanding, well not
really, but the space in between our galaxies is getting
farther and farther and darker and darker so i guess
kinda our universe is becoming smaller and smaller in
perspective to everything which is nothing, wait..

the only thing that is not a rambling of randomness
can be found in one another, where nights that are too
hot to sleep, is this just a *rambling* of consciousness
or unconscious or who knows i am not a psychology
major, when you think about it all and by all i mean
it all is just a rambling of maybe meaning in the
seemingness

-i am a business major because i conformed to the
ideal of success that leads to nowhere
except where we have been as money is not happiness
but as i am told leads to happiness for if you are not
wealthy then you are not rich and if you are not rich
then white and i am white but i hate it because it is too
bright for my permanently dilated eyes that i had eye
surgery on to help me see straight which did not work
because i still see things as crooked/ wicked/ sickened/

can i lay my nose here for a few days
the political shambles is constricting the oxygen as
everything is going to shit
if only going away could allow time to heal
yet healing is in itself a detonation and deterioration
as razors rust

the dust never settles

my ceiling fan shakes when i turn it on full speed
- teaming with memorization - minimization of
blameless decoration

wondering is numbing/ consuming/ drug
inducing; if the colors of the nation's carpet
could change/ if you do this then you can finally
be happy/ convinced to coexist among
heartless patriarchs/ i cinched a harness

to picking at a hangnail on my thumb

twisting beautiful into a friendship
bracelet for nighttime daydreams -
sexual contortion of the mind - what am i
when what am i is not who am i
despite what the misunderstood fall into via default -
it is not your FAULT
that some of this world chooses not to love you.

eating ice cubes as a pastime
tracing trembling roots to their origin
i am afraid of the dark because i am being followed/
watched/ glared at/ stepped on/ choked/ stuffed to sit
pretty on the shelf of *freedom* - leaking with leeches of
desire.
-the greasier the better-

raised upon
no comment

died upon
red cement

comparison is the death of self love/ comparison is
the enemy of blue sky which i don't like for i always
get sunburned as i am a white male and we deserve
it *dont we/* comparison is the reason for personal
abandonment for a strangers judgement/ comparison
is the six pack and abs that self worth is addicted to/
comparison is the emptiness in self and the hallow
adoption of others/

Tallinn, Estonia - 09/10/2022

i turn 20 in 2 days - stagnant obsessions are held on my eyebrows like the beads of sweat from holding up the weight of sunsets each night - i played with cars until i played with cancer - i slept in my parents bed until i was 10 - maybe because we never lived in one place for too long and i lived out of a backpack for 18 years - my therapist says that doesn't matter when you are a normal boy and i am a normal boy who likes playing catch but i can never catch my breath from all of the action movies.

informality is the mitochondria of vulnerability - in Freshman year of high school nobody talked to me because i was forced to be vulnerable- it doesn't feel honorable when you do not have a choice to battle - before i battled my body - **now i battle the way the air hugs my hand when i stick it out the window while driving 90 mph.**

for life is always going too fast or not fast enough

we don't even say hello,
you don't respond,

doesn't that bother you?

postpone - postpone - cut the grass - metallic virtues
at my heels - biting - clawing - slithering to the next
guy

please do be cautious about what you say around me
because i am delicate and i break easy even though i
don't look dented at all - i wish for my love to not be
for rent - or mortgaged - because these days prices are
so damn high - jumping rope with recession - for let's
just admit this obsession as normal despite what god
might say to you if he ever found out what you really
were...

my clothes are uNcOMftoRBLe
so are yoU
that does not make **inequality a justice**

my lips are chapped from thinking about saying what i am thinking about feeling - TWEAKING- no i actually do not do drugs because i do prescriptions and that is enough to swallow

i stopped at a gas station and bought some mint
chapstick for the road
i hate fucking mint chapstick

birthdays send me through forgettance - call me
maybe - if you remember
my name - not distrubing - the shadows orbit with
graceful dissonance like ballerinas on concrete- feeble
resonance/ mental indignation/ rancid allocations of
agelessness/ tally up the score between you and...

blame is ignorance dressed up for high school
graduation/ follow in sentimental elimination of
saturation - it is Saturday, relax, enjoy - rest up for the
next 50 years of clocking in and out, in and out, in and
out, and then out once more.

is this it and by it i mean it all and
by it all i mean everything and by everything i mean
your purpose here in this pile of dust of that insseem
everyday - order up - equality is LATE again - with
some extra napkins to clean up the mess

to confess is to succumb to arbitrates/ when
foundations leak into evolving insanity/ left over from
a fancy restaurant and never touched again - that
smell is your individuality/ resume the regime and
don't move on - parenthood where did you
go ?

solutions:
not in the science sort of way but the unavoidable and unachievable
15 minutes turns into a lifetime of staining wood for a future without the loveclub
-flipping/ tables-

rituals

driving my prius on a rutted dirt road
to arrive at a place only spoken about
-as the soul had imagined-
wonder is a waterfall of preposterous immensity
immune to the density of the human heart
stolen iron - stainless steel appliances will line my
home - that is.

will anyone ever collect the pieces - as in i do not like
reeses peanut butter cups - as in the average person -
as in a fundamental
concept
of

-reclining sensibility

why do i need to be a what and why is there always a
what to every who
what is whom you are destined to be as deemed
by society - a society that has abandoned reality
at its finest - by what i mean is a society that has
loosened the reins on humanhood so far that we have
forgotten what it means to remain human - or that is
assuming things

leave me alone

be you they said,
but then they dispose of you

they never meant it

but i mean it

sorry

Stavanger, Norway - 10/12/2022

listen to:
-'Hide' by Rainbow Kitten Suprise

i met gasoline in the park that a boy once played

.love is not to be fucked with.

double yellow - crossing over pasteurized punctuation
- bloodless backwash brimming - boiling - burning
intestines - morbidity at its finest - using plastic
spoons to dig a hole into enemy territory - my organs

paraphrase the pastel princess/ transparent prince.
as exhibitions.
cursing the carpet for the footprints it leaves behind.
smothering trash can liners that hold the waste.
to-get-her
to please him
when him should be we
according to the matching game

work meeting: date June 22nd 2022 8:03 am

distortion is an infestation of casual
may attraction forever haunt unspoken aspen trees

windless wind chimes still speak

running water plugs my ears/ floods who i am/ this
canyon/ twelve miles deep/ to see some dirt and water
mix

this is as you are not seeming to understand urgent
for me to go and do and be this unknown/ fear/ i dont
want to/ i wish you could talk to me/

my texts have been begging you for help/ for support/
for love/ on this journey and you keep postponing/
delaying/ pushing off/ pushing away/ the reality

do you understand me?

Roe v Wade was overturned
-June 24th 2022

at dinner god told me my choice in love was morally
questionable but you said it was not what he meant
but he did not correct himself and i know he wishes i
could correct me too

people choose to dislike you for your body. for the parts
of you you had no influence in designing because you
are no artchitect and yet you are still bolted to the wall
waiting waiting waiting. for the truth to not hurt your
head so god damn bad. i clean my body over and over
hoping that the next time i look in the mirror i will see
something new/ someone new/ another body/ another
skin/ a different mind that's the one that makes it so
hard to talk about me going away from you

can't you see i am doing this on my own
-quivering

"i have seen them"
"one of them lives next to me"

those queer kids

i don't play these games - paint splotches on the floor - observing the fun precariously from a distance - as mislabeled - as mistreated -

HOW IS EVERYONE
ACTING SO NORMAL when equal rights are
being taken away by STRAIGHT white men in power/
HOW IS THIS ANOTHER
DAY/ HOW HAS THE
WORLD NOT STOPPED AND SAID APRIL FOOLS

"this kids look sicker than last week", do you mean the
kids look more sick than last week and to that i say
why yes yes we do because we have no rights to our
own eyes, what you see is what i get and no return

i dont drink soda but i want a coke
for nothing seems to matter these days except the
future and the past which are forever gone

i clean the bathrooms that are still clean from
yesterday and the day before and before that and the
one before that

this is the way my body sees itself
this is the way some old white men try to bury my life
with their fallacy

we are in danger.
new page, new light
new age, old fight
we are in danger

the familiar taste of blood

open your jaw too wide

reside is religious persecution

familiar irresolution

preset destination

GO

frozen fascination - exchanged for corrupted
commemoration
oh bless this inauguration

i am not here
i am sitting here, doing nothing, in this bottle necked day
listening, watching, waiting for more to be taken
freedom is heard not enacted
i am not here
because i can write until my heart turns black but
none of these words will mean anything to the men
sitting on their asses watching as life turns sour for
those they will never touch

"i will pray for you"
can you pray for the eyes of god to love me in the
same way as they love straight white men
can you pray for the women who are being stripped
their natural beings
can you pray for the men in the suits who apparently
think it is funny to make equality a standing joke

I WILL PRAY FOR YOU TO BE ABLE TO
COMPREHEND YOUR OWN WRONGDOINGS
YOUR OWN HATREDS
YOUR OWN DISGUST
YOUR OWN SINS

And most of all I WILL PRAY FOR MYSELF to be here

hello

Bern, Switzerland - 08/16/2022

the clouds slept in this morning
cuddling with Rocky Mountain jagged peaks

fog fills me with protection/ a rejection of everything
above you/

early morning bird calls
the river seems to be moving slow today
i can't help falling in love with anybody that speaks my
name

connections, it is always about fucking connections

June 29th 2022
i got my wisdom teeth pulled yesterday and i
think i took too many painkillers
sign your life away
"what sexual orientation do you identify with?"
irritation is a natural feeling around strangers

i should have taken Freshman year honors English
vocabulary more seriously
sit up straight
big biceps = manly = desirable = loved = ihatemyself =
iamjustkidding

the surgeon told me to swish salt water in my bloody
gum sockets 3-5 times a day
i said okay

———

what about the women
what are we doing to clean the tyranny in
the land of the free

the truth makes me drowsy
boyishness in the Supreme Court
controlling a state of false consciousness with a
revolver
wake me up when the war is over/ i tried to sleep in
but my anxiety opened my eyes at 7 pm before i even
fell asleep/

constant confliction of attraction - why am i still
fighting this - there is not choice but life - you are
what you are because i said so -
there is somebody upstairs in my house

at work a bunny followed me. it ate the little white
flowers or maybe they are technically weeds.   then it
hopped on

the fucks i would give to hop on
            to a new meadow with brighter flowers
                                    there was a fire here, which
leaves the best soil for new agriculture
                                    for the economy and the
stock market   invest
now and be rich later

you called me twice today
i watched my phone ring
paralyzed in peril

'i am no Ferris Beuller'
it is too late to save Ferris

is it too late for the world to work itself out
are we too fucked for our own good
are their eyes platonic or mutiny

independence day 2022:
human me - ruin the ending of every Disney movie -
undoing - the fundamental of doing when wrongdoing
is the state of normalcy - *morally questionable* - deem
me underneath crumbling bridges - your background
- homage.

untangle, untangle, untangle, to tangle, and untangle
some more

forcing.
.picture perfect.
evaporate and reform
torn gender
worn blue for the morally dictating
.restricting.

-wrapping presents-

born beautiful
taught to self cripple
my rights and lefts are subject to eyeliner
objective blank skin tones
'why'

humanity is not a profanity

when bones are little, swords are strong
emptiness is an empress that was left on read

ghosted by the government
again

what if i dyed my hair teal/ would the world change
how they feel about men like me/
no exceptions!

there are no receipts
keeping tallies for the rallies/ petitions/ recessions/
depressions/ concussions/ intersections don't mix
when words don't stick

swipe away your destiny
to the Fourth of July fireworks

such lovely barbarians
such colorful criminals

hey, it is me
again
none of this music sounds good anymore
without you
mildew in modernity
malice in justice
may i have this dance...
the song gets louder the longer it plays
i miss you
circulating content with crayons
shading in lost lines
remininants of soft needles
searching thunder
i am listening to the smell of the rain
it reminds me
repeating in the back of my throat
another day receding
fumbling imagination, silly boy
make it go away.

skewed perception plastered on bare skin. barbed wire

i will never know my own body

use caution in each other/ abrasions leaves scars/
playtime in the judiciary/ overturning cul de sacs-
replacing suburbia in disturbia

constant collision
between sentience
burning fossil fuels to cure cancer
color in the boy in
remembrance is absence
going to bed early
stranger love than this
B-A-G-G-A-G-E
psychotic emotions
edging cornerstone

because i am not beautiful
i get scared at night from the looming light
i am not sane unless there is rain
because downpour is ugly
and i am not beautiful
i cover my mouth to internalize the system
to become the system
so i don't cry into the gears and cause it
to rust and leak
because i am not beautiful
and i like it that way
for beauty has been muting me
but you can never silence the sea
before it floods and knocks down
the doorways that once stood out of principle
now life rafts
that will soon begin to splinter apart
as my body does when i see a reflection
or close my eyes a little too tightly

it is too loud in here
and i was just trying to sleep but now i am editing my mistakes
as if i could take anything back and change it
but i can't
because i was never beautiful
and when i saw you driving the other day
i wished i wasn't so terrified to be happy
happiness has no space for a fool like me
and that ceramic pot i bought you broke in my bag

eventhough i wrapped it three times with bubble wrap
and placed it between a blanket and pillow and i guess
what i am saying is that even when you are being
careful things can still break and fall apart
because i guess i am not beautiful and that
is the end of it
we are all just embarrassments for what it means
to be human
unlike his salt and her flower
we can never be beautiful because we are too busy
cleaning up the pieces of the reckless before us

it is too cold in here
because i am not beautiful

you DESERVE love
you DESERVE equality
you DESERVE truth

the WEIGHT of the world is not your responsibility
the HURT you feel is valid
the DAMAGE done is real

you DESERVE to be yourself
you DESERVE to be protected

simplicity disguised in construction
new apartments glitter in government workers sweat
glass of ice water to wash down contamination

my alarm rings in imitation of fresh cut grass in a
suburban neighborhood just outside of Chicago
stainless steel warms my heart
from packaging to distribution

may your tremor be a contribution to society

dieting is the only way to learn how to abandon
yourself
"a day off"
phone call - phone call - phone call
ring ring it is demise - your demise
but first can i get a squeeze of lemon in my water

medically induced/ pathologically reduced/ vocal
manipulations consume any alterations/

discomfort is a fiberglass that stagnates humanhood
honor is individualism

don't accuse the applesauce they fed you

knock knock
my heart is a stranger
at the door
i never chose
the peep hole was always there but i didn't dare look
through to
the backside of destiny

don't accuse yourself for their human disobedience
absent companionship
the doorbell
it is ringing for change
for revolution
for resolution
equality should not be a needed evolution
not a privilege
just a thing
that is real

a cow hit my car today
driving to work
it pissed and shit right in front of me

bland iced coffee
assaults my culture
old friends - replicated clothing
nothing was ever told correctly

i saw you walking down the street
i could not believe i didn't recognize you
in the same overalls you wore back in high school
back when we never thought we would be here, now.

what did you think of me when you saw me

it was different there
it is different now

inbetweens alter before my eyes can blink away the confusion

words are sand paper
to tarnish chains laced upon
eccentricity
equal inconsistency is formidable - lethargy

i am terrible at parking
correct is crooked
when paper napkins are not suitable to soak up the
bits and pieces of a nation sagging
outside of its own farm

mocked by a little boy
about being
gullible

writing is rejection
living is rejection
as perfection remains fleeting
sipping milk through a plastic straw in a strip
mall of America

i request a new brain
i settle for new slip on vans

accuse and refuse
-non recyclable-

unless there are outcasts buried within the European
pastries and stolen passports
i am from Canada where the ground is cold but people
are warm

-turning the wrong way on a one way street

everything i touch fades to gray
packing boxes in a basement
to be mailed far from those calluses

care to classify the gravity
the flowers stimulate my allergies

coughing up your throat
laced with political determination
for elimination

i think the lightning is following me
driving into fog with cruise control
GET OUT

walk with me

i know you more than you ever will
i am you more than you will ever be
walk with me

GET OUT
of your mind your body misses your touch
feel it drip down yours eyes
melt onto your tongue

GET OUTSIDE
of what they call you
and just walk with me

when curiosity becomes too strong
the world seems small compared to the possibilities of
the rain

Edinburgh, Scotland - 12/13/2022

i got a hundred tiny paper cuts in my thumb from
counting paper
the pages my mind uninhabitable
the tree that only grows when you look away

constantly cleaning the dirt out of the planets core
bleaching tides "for the better"
according to whose eyes

rereading daily horoscopes from 5 years ago
still interpreting the trembles of a solemn heart
that broke itself 5 years ago

a nation consuming its body
few constricting the individual

doing favors till the world ends

our eyes caught like a rough part of a fingernail

even though you no longer know me do you still see
me as the boy your played cars with
the one who you listened to Maroon 5 with on repeat
on your bedroom floor

we were so immune to the carbon dioxide

eating hi-chews from the Everything store
riding our bikes like we owned the future

-once upon a time we were best friends.
now we are gone.

memories come in droplets   that lead to rivers

another summer escaped with the flamelight

it's not a date but were not friends
and neither of us really know what we are or who we
are to be exact and i am really just tired of hearing this
day in the back of my brain

it's all a scam

rest your body
for the turmoil
is nonstop

sleep in.

powdered doughnuts on a cliff's edge
sunset is coming

when i looked into her light
across the aching hillsides

impulsively deleting
i tell you my sins so you don't have to

eventually someone will thank me for my honesty
even if it only causes trouble

time out
can we put homophobia in a time out please

-you got the wrong number

bits and pieces

Móns Klint, Denmark - 09/16/2022

amino acids/ big muscles are masculinity
drink my desire dry

another highschool tv show

another exclusion
blue nail polish

-home alone

stop staring at me.   i cant take it.
          my expectations are evaporating.
i picture you wearing sandals but that is not me.
          i wear a pair of shoes until they die.

you wore me until i died

-cool kids

alternatives are blinding me

skin to skin contact is supposed to erase lonelinesses.
but pleasure is not equted to happiness.
and spotify told me i was drepressed.

if you were interested in me
maybe the world could be different

-graphing parabolas

i need a new razor to get a clean shave
these political remnants have me dizzy
reality has a sick sense of humor
the talk of the town is my love life
the most knowledgeable and powerful people are
debating whether or not to codify same-sex marriage
undoing generations of advocacy
ignorance is superior to apathy
this is happening because of rotten roots
it is not your fault, i promise
-a slanted day

sunset picnics are for friends too
            grappling with sandstone
               grabbing for a hand
                  fading compassion and headlines

"reaching an all time high in what the fuck is going on".
i do not understand why it has to be this way.

carrying iced coffee and coffins to work tomorrow.

you do not need to worry about me anymore
i am all grown up

you need to worry about "America"
it's still a child

i am not ready
i am too busy writing poetry

-i do not know what you are doing

justice is not meant to imprison
the innocent
the only people not innocent are...

bit by bit
and piece by piece
we will get there
    i have not slept through the night in two months
    nature is commandeering my dreams
    and by nature i mean humankind
    and by humankind i mean the villains from
movies that i did not think were real

-as i thought

making love a private entity
mimicking a safe and sound sidewalk
when it rains my shirt turns see through
making hate an acceptable characteristic among
political bargainers

respectfully go back to the factory
there has been a mistake
we are losing the possibility of
an honest world

freshly tarnished and painted nails makes for a perfect
afternoon

it is hailing in your arms
i am withering in your arms
please stop carrying arms

-i do not feel safe

from the day that i met you i stopped being okay
at least in the cubicles eye
hexagons are my least favorite shape -
too symmetrical

-don't hug me with with blood on your hands

"would you go on a date with me"

i miss when running was a freedom instead of a
requirement
recklessness is soothing
the light does not belong to us

it is my last day of corporate work in America
to abide by hierarchical leadership where there are no
circular tables
and isn't the river lovely or lonely

you can be surrounded but remain empty

i cant stop myself
from taking out empty trash bags
to throw away some part of me that
would make me cooler

and this wonderful nation loves to take out the trash

for those who do not abide are shoved to the side for
the nature of their insides

claymation at the core
prince charming cratered into stomachs
marching pride - absorbing doubt on white skin

would you call me back if you had the chance
would the sky tell me my love is not a third wheel

the power we don't elect
electing our freedom as objectifiable
rejectable via perceptionism

heteronormative obsessions
make others death by criticism

this is not a tv show
this is real life

smelling oceans in Colorado

bad at love

biologically broken-hearted
deported a normal life
the Senate is battling over my rights
as if it is their question
to determine my happiness
because i am

bad at love

bitter biology as a bases for BRACKetING

last night i called my dad for what felt like the first time because i needed him and he was there because he knew i needed him and i am crying now because i needed him a long time ago and i am sorry for not calling but i was still damaged and now that i am better maybe we can be better.

going back

Stavanger, Norway - 10/03/2022

two shots of espresso
one fear of losing you
zero apologies
sincerely fucked

you are late
again
pretty soon it will be too late to be late
again

reminders swim in the rain
leaping from droplet to droplet
desperate to stay falling for you

sitting alone in a coffee shop

i will never let go of that part of myself
i will grow it out like a plant that just won't die
          overwatered

you cannot kill what you do not know

still waiting to cry
still walking in circles with two right shoes on
still not yours

stitches holding my skin
to shield the politicians bite

white teeth to smile pretty
for the oppressive camera

blooming on trees   screens
dancing amount screams

-we should frame this one

victimizing oneself is not equated to speaking out
against one's victim hood
painkillers - sins - suffocations - because we live and
don't bother - surgeries
follow the rain clouds hidden behind grief
warning, iCloud storage is almost full/ if you take any
more photographs you will be eternally lost
attractiveness [power] / oceans are shallow / someone
else - irrational and arrogant
zero calories - zero fat - zero carbs - zero love
headphones to drown out a man's whimper / crying is
a health hazard / identity crisis / we cannot afford to
risk the interpretations
doing laundry in my brain to sanitize the toning
"you are not that different / you need to get over it/
you are just normal / you are like everybody else / you
are not special / everyone is fucked just the same/
everyone has adversity / you are not different / you are
no an exception"
"okay."
can you pass the ketchup please

i am leaving to see what the world can be
i am leaving to see who i can be
existing alone. grants disruption. entering fear. forfeits
regrets. tire tracks on the skin. styrofoam imprints
[uninhabitable]. lovely humanism
torrential wonder   it can be   numb
challenging the light in between the shadows

how to quantify loneliness   empty stomachs
flying on espresso   five hours early to possible
            being present with oneself can never be alone
abandon belief systems

do the clouds decide where to wander
does the horizon ever get tired of being so far away
foreign mornings sit comfortably on my tongue
i got lost and overheard someone say 'he is gay' as i
walked by
do the pigeons know they are in Venice
beginning and ending the light in the same seat
believing in who you are cannot come from the place
you persist
have you ever seen a pigeon walk down stairs
bad angles
the beauty in sight is the death of yesterdays
forbidden romance - slow dancing amidst tragedy
i spilled my water on the train and a girl handed me a
napkin although we didn't speak the same
i was expecting circular houses - to fall in love again -
to be reminded of the damage
sleeping under a strangers breath
drinking sweetened cappuccinos
on the train a girl knit an abolish the state shirt in a
black skirt
kindness is beyond language
to sit and observe rather than to see / to embody
above appear / to ask for assistance / to believe in the
beloved
i inhaled for the first time in a Swiss river as the
current swept my feet out from under me
intensity / biological similarities / governmental

heresays / royalty lurks behind common sense.
a man walked up to me and started speaking German.
i wonder what he wanted to tell me.
exchanging moments with strangers. people will
match and frag m e n t. chewed up and spit out.
TAKEN
my heart is full of the things i do not know

we are all performing
acting for them
pretending for a fiction
trading the color of our eyes in replacement of another

dear gatekeepers of attractions
how I wish we could see each other clearly instead of a
muffled, fragmented dose of sensuality
do you remember me, the one you used to be

love is like a hard wood
it moves only one way
and if you try to go against the grain
you may become twisted and knotted

the help has gone out with
          the last pearl of dignity on your forehead

                              DROPPING BOMBS in the ocean
to prove a point
POWER + FEAR + HAPPINESS +SAFETY = FUCKED

-October 5th, 2022

i have trouble concentrating on my education

when it does not teach me about heroisms

clickbait   eradicate   dictate the predicate
                    homeliness mitigation

i am here, and here, has made me ever more aware of
there, but i could never go back there
          where suicide is voluntary and guns reside
                    you never did see   us

-cause it feels like we are going back in time

to transition to good / where good is not financial /
rather human decency / how saving the individual
rescues humanhood / from all mighty capitalism
          tortured planet - i am so sorry to my
tormented body - for being tainted by society's vase
holding together fake flowers - that smell of prison
food

im good
it's great

hell boy is his blood - foolishness lurks in the patients
exhale - im not that way anymore
may i have an alibi please mr president

that success floating out there is melting with the
glaciers
and my 6th grade sex ed never told me what i could be
because i couldn't be

i miss what we were
as i never really did know you
and you never cared enough to try to know me
in the ways that i wish i knew you

i miss the way i thought the daylight danced the entire
night away
as i danced away those self alleged allegations

WHY DOES IT NOT FEEL LIKE ENOUGH?
WHY DO I NOT FEEL LIKE ENOUGH when it is the
way it is...

i woke up today feeling fucked
for some nights i cannot get my eyes to close from
staring at the possibilities of nothing
among the absences of moments
that i lost long ago

reform is a daydream while revolution is a dandelion

-hallowing legislation

talk to me
i do not remember the sound of your voice
but i remember the words you said to me before i
went to bed

talk to me if you are still there...

camping out in heartache
my tongue upset
undermined bodies dancing in bones
in the closet

broken business contaminate lost masculinity
sweet sweet serenity
how each eternity has escaped a prisoners dilemma
who told you i would be here

to become a frameless enterprise of picturesque
contours
dead skin i wait for you to heel in the drizzling
daylight
dwindling consciousness

-flu shots

In Denmark their eyes are not a judge
their hands are not as knives
their voices dig beyond surface tension

my throat rots when talking and talking and talking
and talking about the United States of America
a homeland for insecurity, scrutiny

In Denmark the cobblestone is uneven but thy values
lay firm
in the fires of freedom
washed clean with the rain and dried with the wind

i am no good at confrontation
small comments corrupt and control
fracture and fixate
until there is only a singular narrative left
over from the animosity

i try to let it go
but it comes back to me
and the more i release the tighter it chokes

i wish i could just see this as a couple jokes

they have made my body a public entity
along with the others
i am so sorry

demonic to the culture's eye
don't let go
please

this is not what you started
but it has ended you
before you had the chance to begin

-security checkpoint

i am growing a beard to hide my acne
i am starving to define my masculinity
i am faltering in the picture of *beauty*
i am declining according to this constitution
i am leaving because i am lost

tell me why the leaves change color when they die

pain is rain
reclaiming the streets
all on its own

tell me why i must wait longer

same is rain
bulldozing authenticity
invested by politics

tell me why kids can be so mean
i scream in the rain
enabling / destabilizing
to be their own

my brain has become so crowded it has returned
home as it left

empty

except for you circulating on loop

-the journey is off

rain residue on an airplane's wing

singing lullabies for the moon - my hearts unrest /
restricted

i am going to be gone
into the sunrise - where nightmares are replaced by
realities -
unless you are like me - you will sleep when you are
dead

in the air, we shall fly
a giant metal bird, dare i sigh
sitting, writing feeble rhymes
you came and went with true time
but where is mine

dear generation,
sincerely why

my dreams coming true on this ordinary day

oblivious beauty - on this amateur skyline
turbulence takes over until there must be a four leaf
clover

the sickness does not live alone
concealed in capitalism
tarnish / tarnish / vanquish
accuse / accuse / abuse / misuse

dehumanize betterment from the very first settlement
yield to each constituent
for profit is on the line

-it doesn't have to be permanent

fall in love
with being fucked

your universe begins today
love is not legal - it is life
you are not what they say

rest tonight
revolt tomorrow

with the grace of the sun and fire of the moon
it will be different soon

-i wish i could be so profound

Naxos, Greece - 11/05/2022

Finn Mott is eloquent in his extraction of the disregarded, meanwhile interweaving personal anecdotes, sentience, and the inner turmoils of the mind. Finn plants seeds in the modern reluctances of acceptance for a future of equality. Currently, a senior at Colorado College, Finn is studying poetry, business, economics, and society. Finn writes with more than a love, but a responsibility to offer a voice of support, agency, and of sentiment for those undergoing adversity. In his work, Finn provides a lens toward identity acceptance, love, illness, in an attempt to process the world in which we live.

www.ingramcontent.com/pod-product-compliance
Lightning Source LLC
Chambersburg PA
CBHW050816090426
42736CB00022B/3478
* 9 7 8 1 5 9 0 2 1 6 3 5 4 *